Esther

The Providence of God

Es-NK-SS

**A Bible-Based Study
For Individuals and Groups
Leader's Guide Included**

**Lamplighters International
St. Louis Park, Minnesota, USA 55416
www.LamplightersUSA.org**

Lamplighters International
St. Louis Park, Minnesota USA 55416
Fourth printing – June 2006

Lamplighters International is a Christian ministry that publishes Bible-based, Christ-centered resources.

For additional information about the Lamplighters ministry resources contact:
Lamplighters International 6301 Wayzata Blvd, St. Louis Park, Minnesota USA 55416 or visit our web site at www.LamplightersUSA.org.

ISBN # 1-931372-06-3
Order # - ES-NK-SS

Contents

Introduction   7

1a/b - A New Queen   9
    Esther 1:1-2:18

2a/b - "If I Perish, I Perish"   15
    Esther 2:19-4:17

3a/b - How the Mighty Are Fallen   21
    Esther 5:1-7:10

4a/b - The Providence of God   27
    Esther 8:1-10:3

Leader's Guide   32

The Final Exam   43

How to Use This Study

What is Lamplighters?

Lamplighters is a Christ-centered discipleship ministry that is designed to increase your understanding of God's Word and equip you to serve Him more effectively. Each Lamplighters Bible Study is a self-contained unit and an integral part of the entire discipleship ministry.

This study is comprised of five or ten individual lessons, depending on the format you choose. When you have completed the entire study you will have a much greater understanding of a significant portion of God's Word. You will also have learned several new truths that you can apply to your life.

How to Study a Lamplighters Lesson.

A Lamplighters study begins with prayer, your Bible, the weekly lesson, and a sincere desire to learn more about God's Word. The questions are presented in a progressive sequence as you work through the study material. You should not use Bible commentaries or other reference books until you have completed your weekly lesson and met with your weekly group. When you approach the Bible study in this way, you will have the opportunity to personally discover many valuable spiritual truths from the Word of God.

As you prepare for your lesson, find a quiet place to complete your weekly lesson. Each study (Part "a" or "b") will take approximately thirty minutes to complete. If you are new to Lamplighters materials, you should plan to spend more time on the first few lessons. Your weekly personal study time will decrease as you become familiar with the format. Soon you will look forward each week to discovering important life principles in the coming lessons.

You should write your answers in your own words in the space provided within the weekly studies. We have intentionally provided a significant amount of writing space for this purpose. Include appropriate verse references at the end of your carefully worded and thoughtful answers, unless the question calls for a personal opinion. The answers to the questions will be found in the Scripture references at the end of the questions or in the passages listed at the beginning of each study.

"Do you think" Questions

Each weekly study has a few "do you think" questions. These questions ask you to make personal applications from the Biblical truths you are learning. Make a special effort to answer these questions because they are designed to help you apply God's Word to your life. In the first two lessons the "do you think" questions are placed in italic print for easy identification. If you are part of a study group, your insightful answers to these questions could be a great source of spiritual encouragement to others.

How to Use This Study Guide

The Lamplighters discipleship materials are designed for a variety of ministry applications. They have been used successfully in the following settings:

Self-study - Read the passage listed at the beginning of the weekly lesson. Seek to gain as much understanding from the Text as possible. Answer the questions in the space provided, using complete sentences if the space allows. Complete the entire lesson without looking at the Leader's Guide in the back of the book. Discipline yourself to answer all the questions so that you gain the maximum benefit from the lesson. When you have completed the lesson, read the corresponding portion of the Leader's Guide to gain greater understanding of the passage you have just studied.

One-on-one discipleship - Complete the entire lesson without referring to the Leader's Guide. If you are leading the one-on-one discipleship time meeting, become familiar with the Leader's Guide answers before you meet with the person you are discipling. Plan to meet for approximately one hour to discuss the lesson. If you are not the leader, do not look at the Leader's Guide until you have met for the meeting.

Small Group discipleship - The members of the discipleship group should complete their weekly lessons without referring to the Leader's Guide. The Group Leader should complete the lesson before he becomes thoroughly familiar with the Leader's Guide answers. A comprehensive ministry manual has been prepared for church leaders to help lead small groups effectively and implement the Lamplighters discipleship ministry into their church.

Class teaching (Adult or Senior High Sunday School Classes) - The pastor or teacher should complete the entire lesson before class, review the Leader's Guide answers, and prayerfully consider how to present the lesson. The class members should complete their weekly lessons in advance so that they can bring their thoughtful insights and questions to the class discussion time. The Teacher's Edition makes an excellent companion to this format and allows the teacher to design specific lessons appropriate in length and knowledge level for the students. For more information on combining these two products, contact Lamplighters or visit our website

Personal Questions

Occasionally you will be asked to respond to personal questions that you should do your best to answer. If you are part of a study group, you will not be asked to share any personal information about yourself. However, be sure to answer these questions for your own benefit because they will help you compare your present level of spiritual maturity to the Biblical principles presented in the lesson.

A Final Word

Throughout this study the masculine pronouns are often used in the generic sense to avoid awkward sentence construction. When the pronouns "he," "him," and "his" are used to refer to the Trinity (God the father, Jesus Christ and the Holy Spirit), they always refer to the masculine gender.

This Lamplighters study is presented after many hours of careful preparation. It is our prayer that it will help you **grow in the grace and knowledge of our Lord and Savior Jesus Christ. To Him be the glory both now and forever. Amen** (2 Peter 3:18).

About the Author

John Alexander Stewart was born and raised near Winnipeg, Canada. He was drafted by the Pittsburgh Penguins (NHL) and played professional hockey for eight years. He was born again in 1977 when he accepted Jesus Christ alone for eternal life. He graduated from seminary in 1988. He served as a pastor for fifteen years. During this time he planted two Bible-believing churches. He also founded Lamplighters International and now serves as the executive director of the ministry.

Introduction

Esther is only one of the two books in the Bible named after women. The book of Esther shares an interesting relationship with its counterpart, Ruth. Esther, a beautiful, young, Jewish woman, became queen of the powerful, ancient Persian Empire. She would have lived a life of ease and opulence if a top Persian official had not devised a wicked plan to systematically exterminate her fellow Jews. On the other hand, Ruth, a poor Gentile widow, left her homeland during a famine to glean in the fields of Bethlehem. She would have lived out her remaining years in abject poverty and social obscurity if she had not met and married a godly, elderly landowner named Boaz. Esther and Ruth share a common bond: both were given vital roles in God's sovereign plan and both are remembered for their willingness to trust God during very difficult circumstances. God honored their willingness to trust Him by preserving the books that bear their names.

Historical Background

In 586 BC, Nebuchadnezzar and his Babylonian army sacked and burned Jerusalem, bringing an end to the southern kingdom of Judah and their formal occupation of Palestine. As the prophets Isaiah and Jeremiah fortold many years earlier, the Jewish people, except for the poor, were taken captive to Babylon,. In Babylon, the Jews were allowed to build homes and engage in business. Many of the Jewish people became content in their new environment.

In 539 BC, Babylon was conquered by the Persians, led by Cyrus the Great. During the first year of his reign (538 BC), Cyrus initiated a royal decree that allowed the Jewish exiles to return to Palestine (cf. Ezra 1:1-4) so that they could rebuild the temple and set up the sacrificial system. The first of three groups of Jewish exiles returned under Sheshbazzar's leadership (cf. Ezra 1:1-2:70). A second group, led by Ezra, did not return until 58 years later (cf. Ezra 7:1 ff.). Nehemiah led the third and final group back to Palestine in 444 BC - ninety-four years after Cyrus's original decree. Even though the prophets warned the Jews to return to Palestine (cf. Is. 48:20; Jer. 50:8; 51:6), many chose to reject the words of the prophets and remain in Persia.

The events of the Book of Esther take place in Persia during the reign of Ahasuerus, the fourth king of the Persian Empire (486-465 BC). This means that the events of the book of Esther occur between the first and second major returns of the Jewish people to Palestine. In the Biblical text, this means that the chronological events of the book of Esther can be placed after Ezra six and before Ezra seven. From the internal evidence, the book covers approximately ten years of ancient Jewish history: Ashasuerus's 3rd year, 483 BC, to his 12th year (Es. 1:3; 3:7).

Purpose and Importance

Conservative Biblical scholars have offered several ideas regarding the central theme or purpose of the Book of Esther. Perhaps the most common one is that the book simply describes the origin and administration of the feast of Purim, a sacred Jewish holiday. The Jewish people, living in various parts of the ancient Persian Empire during the time of the actual events of the book, would not have known of God's great deliverance from the hand of Haman without this important record. A second suggested central theme is that the book was originally written to remind the returning exiles of God's faithfulness. According to this view, God's was faithful to the Jewish people in spite of their unwillingness to return to Palestine, substantial evidence of God's continuing love for His people. A third suggested theme is that the book teaches that God's providential care overrules all things in all lands. The diabolical plans of a top-ranking Gentile official who gains the support of the powerful Persian king cannot overcome God's sovereign plan for the affairs of human history and for His people in particular.

Study # 1a   **A New Queen**

1. Give the names of the only two women after whom books of the Bible are named.

    Esther and Ruth

2. Give a brief description of the woman Esther from the **Introduction**.

    Faithful

3. There are some interesting contrasts between Esther and Ruth. Contrast the lives of these two women who were so greatly used by God.

    Esther - Queen, Beautiful

    Ruth - Poor, Widow

4. a. What Gentile nation did God use to chasten the southern kingdom of Judah for their rebellion against Him?

    Babylon

    b. Name two Old Testament (hereafter, "OT") prophets whom God used to warn the Jews about the coming captivity in Babylon?

5. On three different occasions, large groups of Jewish exiles returned to Palestine. Name the three Jewish leaders who led the various expeditions.

    1. Sheshbazzar   2. Ezra   3. Nehemiah

6. a. When and where do the actual events of the Book of Esther occur?

Persia

    b. If you were asked to place the events of the Book of Esther within the chronology of the Book of Ezra, where should they be placed?

7. How do we know that the actual events of the Book of Esther occupy approximately ten years of Jewish history?

8. Conservative Bible scholars have suggested three purposes or central themes for the original writing of Esther. What are they?

Study #1b   **A New Queen**

Read - Introduction, Esther 1:1-2:18; other references as given.

9. The book of Esther begins with the introduction of King Ahasuerus of Persia, also known by the Greek name Xerxes, who ruled over 127 provinces (Es. 1:1-2). Ahasuerus was a powerful king whose kingdom extended from India (present-day Pakistan, but not the southern peninsular of India) to Ethiopia (Heb. *Cush*- the upper Nile region corresponding to present-day southern Egypt and northern Ethiopia). What significant event took place in the third year of his reign (Es. 1:3-4)?

    Banquet for all his nobles

10. It seems hard to believe that anyone, even a powerful Persian king, could host a royal banquet that lasted 180 days. The Greek historian Herodotus (485-425 BC) informs us in his *History* that Ahasuerus was planning an invasion of Greece to avenge the shameful defeat and death of his father at the Battle of Marathon in 490 BC. Persian princes and other military leaders would have come to the Persian capital of Susa at various times during the banquet to become convinced of Ahasuerus's wealth and to plan the invasion of Greece. What two things happened after the 180 days were completed (Es. 1:5, 10)?

    for all in the citadel and 7 day banquet to present Queen Vashti.

11. On the seventh and final day of Ahasuerus's banquet for the people of Susa and Vashti's banquet for the women in the palace, he commanded seven servants to bring Vashti to his banquet, but she refused (Es. 1:12).

    a. Why did Ahasuerus want Vashti to come to his banquet?

        Display her beauty to the people and nobles

    b. How did Ahasuerus respond to Vashti's refusal to come to his banquet (Es. 1:12-15)?

        He became furious and dethroned her.

12. Ahasuerus was able to control the entire Persian Empire but he was not able to control his own spirit or his own family. The Bible says, **"Whoever has no rule over his own spirit is like a city that is broken down, without walls."** (Pro. 25:28).

   a.   In what ways *do you think* a man who has no control over his spirit is like a city that is broken down and without walls?

   Enemies can control, no boundaries, no structure

   b.   Have you allowed God to take control of your spirit so that you are not like a city broken down and without walls? YES, it was not easy though

13. Ahasuerus and Vashti allowed an interpersonal disagreement to become a national scandal. In the same way Christian churches often allow personal problems with others to become "national" issues.

   a.   What *do you think* Ahasuerus could have done to prevent the problem from becoming a major issue? Love her, don't treat her like an object, fill her in on the plan

   b.   What *do you think* Vashti could have done differently to resolve the problem and not dishonor her husband? Respectfully request "to not to", Come but discuss this at another time

14. Ahasuerus asked the wise men what they thought should be done with Vashti (Es. 1:15). Fearing that her example might cause widespread contempt within the homes of the Persian Empire, they advised the king to divorce Vashti and marry another, more worthy than she (Es. 1:16-19). Although Ahasuerus took their advice and had Vashti deposed, he later regretted his foolish, hasty decision (Es. 2:1).

    a. In the Book of Esther, many people received counsel from others (cf. Es. 2:22-23; 3:13-15; 4:14; 6:6-9). Although the Bible encourages believers to seek counsel from others, it cautions them to receive only godly counsel (Pro. 1:4; 24:6). When *do you think* a Christian should not accept the counsel of other people? *Does not follow what the bible lays out*

    b. How can a Christian be sure that the counsel he receives from another person is godly counsel (Isaiah 8:20)? *Measure what is said against the word*

15. Perhaps the king's attendants (probably the wise men of Esther 1:13-14) feared that Ahasuerus might reinstate Vashti as queen (Es. 2:1). What plan did they offer the king so that a new queen might be chosen (Es. 2:2-4, 12-14)? *Beautiful virgins*

16. Esther was taken into Ahasuerus's harem to prepare herself for twelve months before being presented to the king (Es. 2:8, 12). During this time, she found favor with Hegai, the king's eunuch, who was in charge of the king's harem (Es. 2:3, 8-9). By law Esther was not to marry a pagan (De. 7:1-4) nor was she to have sexual relations with a man before marriage (Ex. 20:14). What evidence does the text offer that Esther did not willingly volunteer for this responsibility (Es. 2:3, 8)? *She had to be a virgin*

17. When the prophet Daniel was taken to Babylon, he refused to defile himself by eating the king's choice food (Dan. 1:8). The three Hebrew youths refused to bow down to the king's statue (Dan. 3:13-18). However, several years after Daniel, Esther apparently had no qualms about the food she ate in the palace (Es. 2:9). In addition, Mordecai instructed her not to reveal her Jewish identity. What *do you think* this indicates about the faith of Mordecai and Esther?

It indicates nothing beyond a sentence of an entire story. You're asking me to judge.

18. Among all the beautiful women of the Persian Empire, Esther was chosen to become queen (Es. 2:17). Little did she realize at the time that God had placed her in a strategic position within the kingdom so that He might use her in a mighty way. Give a personal example of how God providentially directed your life then used you for His glory.

My job, IT Mgr, my wife, my mother

BEN - house was robbed, Ashley - day care, BEN BRYAN - PE

SEAN + BONNIE BELLIVEAU

Psalm 119:105 *"Your word is a lamp to my feet and a light to my path."*

Study # 2a   *"If I Perish, I Perish"*

Read - Esther 2:19-4:17; other references as given.

1. Esther, a physically beautiful young Jewish woman, became the queen of Persia. How do we know that she possessed a measure of inner beauty as well (Es. 2:19-20)? *She is faithful, obedient, and long suffering*

2. Although the Book of Esther does not directly mention the name of God, His providential working (i.e., working through secondary means to bring about His divine will on earth) is clear in orchestrating the affairs of human history. Vashti was deposed, and Esther was chosen to be queen ahead of all the women of the empire. What other evidences of God's providential working are apparent in the development of the book at this point (Es. 2:21-23; 6:1-3)? *Esther's dinner, Haman's demise, King not being able to sleep*

3. Some Biblical commentators believe Esther used her position as queen to secure an appointment of Mordecai as a lower magistrate or judge. (Note: The Text mentions Mordecai sitting at the gate, where justice was dispensed, five times: 2:21, 3:2, 5:9, 13, 6:10, 12; [cf. Ru. 3:1-11].) If this was the case, Mordecai would have been in an excellent position to receive news of two trusted officials plotting to assassinate the king (Es. 2:21-22).

   a. Neither Esther nor Mordecai were aware that God had directed them into specific positions to be used for His glory. What important truth(s) do you think this teaches about the way God works in the lives of His people? *His ways are too great, He is faithful when we are not, He does not give us more than we can handle*

b.   In what way(s) do you think these truths should affect your trust in God?

Complete and utter faith

4.   Sometime later, King Ahasuerus promoted a wicked official named Haman and gave him authority over all the nobles of the empire (Es. 3:1). Haman was an Agagite which could mean he came from a Persian district named Agag (archeologists have found an inscription attesting to this fact) or it could mean that he was descendant of Agag, king of the Amalekites (1 Sam. 15:58).

a.   During the exodus from Egypt, whom did the Amalekites attack among the Israelite pilgrims (Deut. 25:17-18)?   *Weary and worn out*

b.   What did God tell the Israelites to do to the Amalekites after they (the Israelites) were firmly established in the Promised Land (Deut. 25:19)?   *Blot out the memory of Amalek from under heaven*

5.   God (and the prophet Samuel) commanded Saul, the first king of Israel to destroy the Amalekites for their wickedness against Israel during the Exodus (1 Sam. 15:1-3; 17-24). Saul failed to obey the Word of the Lord then lost his crown and his life. Bible teachers have often used Benjaminite Saul as an example of someone who is tolerant of evil or sin. They say the believer must gain victory over sin in his life or it will plague him continually and eventually defeat him.

a.   How did Saul die (2 Sam. 1:1-10)?   *At the hand of an Amalekite*

b.   Is there an "Amalekite" in your life—some sinful habit that you know is wrong, but are rationalizing in your mind?

6. What can a believer expect if he is not willing to defeat sinful habits in his life through the power of God (Ja. 1:15)? *Death*

7. Haman's new position meant that the king's servants had to bow down to him (Es. 3:2). However, Mordecai, a Jew, was not willing to bow down to Haman (Es. 3:3-4). What rationalizations could Mordecai have used to justify bowing down to Haman?

    Obey those that rule over you, death

8. When Haman saw **"that Mordecai did not bow or pay him homage, Haman was filled with wrath"** (Es. 3:5).

    a. What similarities do you notice between the way Haman reacted to this problem and the way Ahasuerus dealt with Vashti's unwillingness to attend the royal banquet (Es. 1:12-22; 3:5-11)? *Quick to anger, no love,*

       no dialogue as to why

    b. What important principles do you think these two situations (i.e., Ahasuerus's and Haman's approach to interpersonal conflict resolution) teach us about leadership? *People will follow those who are just,*

       Anger will only lead to bad decisions

Study # 2b   *"If I Perish, I Perish"*

Read - Esther 2:19-4:17; other references as given.

9.   Haman was a little man (in character) who became a top government official. He offered the king a bribe to further his political desires (Es. 3:8-9). Unlike Daniel, who served in a similar position some sixty years earlier, Haman abused his power and sought to destroy the people he was supposed to serve.

   a.   What additional evidence is given to show that King Ahasuerus was a man of poor character (Es. 3:10-15)?

   b.   The British essayist Walter Landor (1775-1864) wrote, "When little men cast long shadows, it is a sign that the sun is beginning to set." Do you believe that men of little character are having an increased influence on America? Why or why not?

10. When Mordecai learned about the king's commandment to destroy, kill, and annihilate all the Jews (Es. 3:13), he and other Jews throughout the kingdom dressed in sackcloth and put ashes on their heads to demonstrate their distress (Es. 4:1-3; cf. Gen. 37:34; Dan. 9:3; Jon. 3:6). Mordecai likely went to the king's gate dressed in sackcloth and ashes hoping to attract Esther's attention (Es. 4:4). What happened when Mordecai refused the clothes that Esther sent (Es. 4:5-6)?

11. Esther sent her servant Hathach to determine the exact nature of Mordecai's distress. Mordecai took the opportunity to relay valuable information to Esther through her servant (Es. 4:7-8).

    a. There were three important pieces of information that Mordecai asked Hathach to relay to Esther. What were they (Es. 4:7-8)?

    b. What did Mordecai order Esther to do (Es. 4:8)?

12. Esther's first response to Mordecai's distress was to send him garments so he could change his clothes (Es. 4:4). Rather than deal with the root cause of the problem, she simply wanted Mordecai to discontinue his mourning. What was her second method of handling this critical problem (Es. 4:10-11)?

13. Many people try to resolve their problems by changing their surroundings (buying new clothes, putting on a happy face, etc.) or by simply avoiding the problem. They believe that the risk of personal injury is simply too much to justify their involvement. Edmund Burke, the British politician, has been generally credited with the statement, "All that is required for evil to triumph is for good men to do nothing."

   a. Mordecai instructed the king's servants to tell Esther four things that would show her her need to help solve the problem. What are they (Es. 4:13-14)?

   b. What did she want Mordecai and the Jews of Susa to do before she approached the king with her request (Es. 4:16)?

14. God brought Esther to the kingdom for such a time as this (Es. 4:14), but she also needed a surrendered heart before He could use her. What did Esther say that indicated she was willing to be His servant (Es. 4:16)?

Psalm 119:105 "Your word is a lamp to my feet and a light to my path."

Study # 3a   How the Mighty Are Fallen

Read - Esther 5:1-7:10; other references as given.

1. On the third day of fasting, Esther dressed in royal apparel and presented herself before King Ahasuerus (Es. 5:1-2). Even though the king had not seen Esther in a month (Es. 4:11), he held out his golden scepter signifying his approval of her visit. What did Ahasuerus say to her (Es. 5:3)? *Whatever your request*
up to half of the kingdom if you wish.

2. The king's response, **"it shall be given to you – up to half the kingdom"** (Es. 5:3) is reminiscent of King Herod's response to Herodias's daughter (cf. Mk. 6:23). Since ancient oriental monarchs held a relatively low opinion of women, it seems unlikely that this offer should be interpreted literally. What do you think the king meant (Es. 5:3)? *Elohim, 6 were going to be given to the elect*

3. The Lord gave Esther strength to approach the king despite her apprehension for the encounter (cf. Es. 4:11, 16). Similarly, many believers tend to avoid other believers who make them feel uncomfortable. When they do this, they violate the Biblical standard that God has established for His people.

    a. How does the Bible describe the relationship that Christians should have toward one another (1 Pe. 1:22)? *Love, kindness, sincere love*

    b. Are you avoiding another believer (in your church, neighborhood, place of employment, etc.) because of fear or discomfort?

4. Sometimes God withholds His blessing from a church ministry because believers within the assembly are unwilling to love one another. Rather than trusting God for strength as Esther did, they resist the grace of God and quench the Spirit's work in their hearts. What counsel would you give a Christian who realized that he was sinning against God by subtly avoiding another believer? *In all kindness and loving ability rebuke them and spur them to contact that other believer*

5. Esther invited the king and Haman to a banquet that she had already prepared for him (Es. 5:4). Her request was unusual because the king and the queen would normally eat in different parts of the palace complex. What do you think Esther's early preparation of the meal indicated about her faith? *cooked meal? She believed in a well She might have used that time ask for blessings.*

6. During the first banquet, King Ahasuerus displayed patience and kindness by not demanding that Esther tell him the nature of her problem. No doubt Esther appreciated his patience and realized her need to assure the king that she was not "putting him off" indefinitely. List three things that Esther said to the king that assured him that she would soon explain the problem (Es. 5:8). *- pleases the King to grant her petition and request - come to my banquet tomorrow - then she will answer the king*

7. Although Haman happily left the first banquet, he was quickly filled with anger when he saw Mordecai in the king's gate (Es. 5:9). However, he controlled himself and went to his house (Es. 5:9-10). List five things that Haman boasted about to his wife and friends (Es. 5:11-12). *- wealth - sons - kings honors - position - only person Queen Esther invited*

8. God had providentially blessed Haman's life (family, riches, etc.) despite Haman's refusal to acknowledge God's authority over his life. Until a man acknowledges that all he has comes from the Lord's benevolence, he cannot truly be content.

   a. What did Haman say about his good fortune (Es. 5:13)?

   Doesn't do him any peace as long as the Jews live.

   b. What did King Solomon say about all he had acquired for selfish reasons (Ecc. 2:8-11, 24-26)?

   Nothing was gain

   c. The apostle Paul said that he had learned to be content (Phi. 4:11). Have you learned to be content with what God has given you, or are you still striving to find satisfaction in the things you possess or control?

9. King Ahasuerus received bad advice from his counselors (Es. 1:14-21), and Haman received bad advice from his wife and friends regarding his problem with Mordecai. What was wrong with their advice (Es. 5:14)?

   They did not seek out and discuss with the people what the problem was.

Study # 3b How the Mighty Are Fallen

Read - Esther 5:1-7:10; other references as given.

10. Many people, including some Christians, regard God's providence as mere coincidence or good fortune.

    a.   Give at least three instances of God's providential care for His people that others might regard as only good fortune or luck (Es. 5:1-14).

        David + Goliath

    b.   Give four more instances of God's providence as seen in Esther 6:1-3.

        Bring the book of the records   Read the book
        It was written   It was found

11. Haman was a proud man who was easily angered when others did not honor him (Es. 3:5; 5:9). Proud people are often angry because their self-centered perspective causes them to become easily offended by others. Besides anger, what other negative effects of pride do you notice in Haman's life (Es 6:6-12)? *Egotistical, Short-sighted,*

    Don't seek wise council

12. Ancient Persian religions made much of omens and signs. Rather than relying on the objective truth of God's revelation to man, the Persians considered both fate and chance important in everyday living.

    a.   How did Haman's wife, Zeresh, and his friends, interpret the strange turn of events that Haman experienced earlier that day (Es. 6:13)? *Death*

b. What do you think are some problems with interpreting life from the perspective of signs, fate, and chance? *We have no control over those things*

13. While Haman's wife and friends were still talking with him, a court official arrived to take him to Esther's second banquet (Es. 6:14). During the second banquet, the king again asked Esther to reveal what was on her heart (Es. 7:2). What was her specific problem (Es. 7:3-4)? *Her people have been sold for death*

14. At this point in the narrative, the tension reaches its climax. Would the king fly into a rage since Esther had not previously revealed her identity to him, or would he become incensed that he had been troubled about something already made law? The king apparently did not make the mental connection between his previous legislative action and Esther's present dilemma and asked her who had done such a despicable thing to his queen and her people (cf. Es. 3:8-14).

a. What did Haman do when Esther revealed to Ahasuerus that he was the enemy (Es. 7:6-8)? *Begged for mercy*

b. What does the Bible teach about those who are merciless in their dealings with other people (Ja. 2:13)? *Where no mercy is shown, none will be given*

15. Haman was executed on the gallows (Heb. *es-* tree, wood timber, gallows, something made of wood) that he had build for Mordecai (Es. 7:10). His own pride had built the gallows on which his life was taken. He had attempted to destroy God's people, so he was destroyed. It has been said that the Jewish people have stood at the graves of all who have tried to destroy them. What does Harbonah's statement to the king reveal about his perspective of the struggle between Haman and Mordecai (Es. 7:9)? *He has eyes*

16. The Bible says, **"Do not be deceived; God is not mocked; for whatever a man soweth, that he will also reap"** (Gal. 6:7). This unchanging principle of sowing and reaping is illustrated throughout the Bible and applies to believers and unbelievers alike.

   a. The patriarch Jacob killed an animal and lied to his father Isaac (Gen. 27:1-29). What did he reap for his sin and deception (Gen. 37:31-35)?

   He was broken as though yoke from Esau's neck

   b. Pharaoh of Egypt commanded the execution of all Hebrew sons (Ex. 1:15-22). What happened to Pharaoh and all the Egyptians who would not submit to God's authority (Ex. 12:29)? *Their first born was killed.*

   c. Is there a specific area of your life in which you are violating God's Word and can expect to reap His chastisement?

Psalm 119:105 "Your word is a lamp to my feet, and a light to my path."

Study # 4a   The Providence of God

Read - Esther 8:1-10:3; other references as given.

1. On the day of Haman's execution, King Ahasuerus gave his entire estate to Esther (Es. 8:1). Persian law gave the state the right to confiscate and to distribute the property of condemned criminals. What reward did King Xerxes give to Mordecai (Es. 8:1-2)? *The signet ring Haman held before him.*

2. Some commentators believe that Esther risked her life a second time when she asked the king to avert Haman's evil scheme to kill the Jews (Es. 8:3-4). What is different about this situation that indicates she probably did not risk her life a second time (Es. 8:3-4; 5:1-2)? *It was not in his court where she approached him*

3. Esther fell on her face, wept, and implored her husband to save her and all her fellow Jews living throughout the Persian Empire (Es. 8:4-6). Instead of simply revoking the original edict, King Ahasuerus instructed Esther and Mordecai to write a second edict that gave the Jews authority to defend themselves (Es. 8:8-12). Why didn't the king simply revoke his previous edict to kill the Jews (Daniel 6:5-15)? *It would not overturn his previous edict retaining his authority.*

4. The king's second edict was hurriedly dispatched to the Jews, satraps, governors, and princes of the provinces (Es. 8:9-10). The text mentions three specific responses to Mordecai's promotion and King Ahasuerus's second edict. What are they (Es. 8:15-17)? *Royal Apparel ↳ Linen ↳ Crown   + The city of Shushan rejoiced*

5. **Fear** (Heb. *pachad*, terror, fear, dread) of the Jews fell on many of the peoples of the Persian Empire. God previously had promised to put this divinely induced fear on other nations (cf. De. 2:25). Which OT nations or peoples experienced the same holy terror (Gen. 35:1-6; Jos. 2:1-11; 5:1)? *Bethel - Canaanites, Jericho - Amorites,*

6. God used the simple faith of Esther and Mordecai to strengthen and encourage all the Jewish people. God does not need an army of courageous saints; He needs only one or two to trust Him to do great things through them in spite of their fears. On another occasion, God used two other individuals, Jonathan (the son of Saul, Israel's first king) and Jonathan's armorbearer to strengthen all Israel (cf. 1 Sam. 13, 14).

    a. Name at least four negative consequences of the Israelites' lack of faith in God to protect them during their struggle with the Philistines (1 Sam. 13:5-13)?

    Saul was killed, God removed power

    b. Jonathan and his armorbearer trusted God and attacked an entire garrison of Philistines. The Lord vindicated their faith and gave them a great victory (1 Sam. 14:6-15). Name at least three positive things that happened as a result of their trust in God (1 Sam. 14:20-22).

    Life, Victory, God's favor

7. The early church trusted God, and He placed this same divine dread on those who observed His power (cf. Acts 5:11). Some Christian leaders believe the modern church has lost its spiritual influence on the unsaved world because it is more interested in entertaining the world and gaining acceptance than being faithful to God.

    a. Besides fear, what words or phrases does the Bible use to describe the reactions of the unsaved to the faith of the apostles and the early NT believers (Acts 2:37; 3:11; 4:1-4, 13; 5:13)? *"cut to the heart", "greatly amazed", "believed", "marveled", "esteemed them highly"*

b. Do you agree that the modern church in America has lost its spiritual power? Why or why not?

8. The first verse in Esther nine is a brief synopsis of the bloody conflict between the Jews and their enemies. The remaining verses of the chapter provide specific details of the battle (vv. 2-16) and the initiation of the Jewish Feast of Purim (vv. 17-32). This communication method (i.e., a summary statement followed by specific details) is common throughout the Bible (cf. Gen. 1:27; 2:18-25; Ju. 1:19-36; Ps 73) and teaches an important spiritual truth about effective communication.

   a. Oftentimes married couples struggle in their relationship because they have never learned to communicate in a Biblical manner. Men are typically satisfied with knowing just the main point of a conversation and are not concerned with details. Women often see details as most important and fail to state the main point at the beginning of the conversation. What negative consequences might a couple experience communicating according to these natural tendencies?

   At least 50% divorce

   b. How could you effectively apply this important Biblical truth in your relationships with members of the opposite sex (e.g., at home, work, church)?

Study # 4b   The Providence of God

9.   God's providential hand protected Mordecai, Esther, and their fellow Jews. The word "providence" comes from the Latin *provideo*, which means to see something beforehand (*pro* - before; *video* - I see). God, in His omniscience, sees the events of the future and divinely orchestrates the affairs of life according to His will. To the unregenerate, providence appears to be nothing more than good luck or mere coincidence. It is also very easy for believers to miss God's providential work on their behalf. List one important evidence of God's providential care for His people that has not yet been mentioned in this study (Es. 9:1; 3:7; Pro. 16:33).

10. Some Bible interpreters find it inconceivable that God's people would kill more than 75,000 people in one day (Es. 9:5-6, 16). It is more inconceivable that there were many people who hated the Jews and would risk their lives to kill the Jews against the king's wishes. On the first day of battle, five hundred of the Jews' enemies were killed in the capital city of Susa, including Haman's ten sons (Es. 9:5-10). To some, the killing of Haman's ten sons and the public display of their dead bodies on the gallows appears to be a vindictive act of brutal revenge (Es. 9:13). Why do you think the Jews did this?

11. Three times the writer of Esther reminds the readers that the Jews did not take any of the spoil in their struggle against Haman the Agagite and his followers (Es. 9:10, 15-16). Why do you think the writer emphasized this point to such a degree (cf. 1 Sam 15:12-23)?

12. The Jews in the provinces finished their fighting on the thirteenth of the month, but the fighting lasted a second day in the capital of Susa (Es. 9:13-15). God's deliverance over Haman and their enemies led the Jews to celebrate their victory with feasting and rejoicing (Es. 9:17-19).

    a. Why did Mordecai make the celebration an annual celebration and tradition for the Jews (Es. 9:20-28)?

    b. Why is this Jewish holiday called Purim (Es. 9:23-27)?

13. Theologian Jaroslav Pelikan said, "Tradition is the living faith of the dead; traditionalism is the dead faith of the living." What do you think Christians can do to ensure that significant spiritual traditions do not become dead religious rituals?

14. The Book of Esther is a book of contrast: Vashti and Esther, Haman and Mordecai, the counsel of Zeresh and the counsel of Mordecai, the power of man and the providence of God.

    a. Haman was a wicked man whose quest for power resulted in the deaths of thousands of people and the destruction of his own family. What does the text say about Mordecai as God increased his authority over others (Es. 9:4; 10:3)?

    b. Choose one of the two main characters (Mordecai and Esther). What specific character quality do you admire most in his or her life? Why?

15. What are the most significant spiritual truths taught in this study of Esther?

Study #1a/b   **A New Queen**

1.   Ruth and Esther.

2.   Esther was a beautiful young Jewish woman who became queen of the powerful ancient Persian Empire. She became the wife of King Ahasuerus, the fourth king of the Persian Empire, who ruled from 486-465 BC.

3.   1.   Ruth was a Gentile, but Esther was a Jew.
      2.   Ruth moved voluntarily to Palestine, but Esther and her people were deported to a foreign land.
      3.   Ruth was an impoverished and barren widow, but Esther was a beautiful, young unmarried woman chosen to be queen of Persia.
      4.   Ruth had the burden of caring for her mother-in-law Naomi, but Esther was cared for by her cousin Mordecai.

4.   a.   Babylon, under the leadership of Nebuchadnezzar.
      b.   Isaiah and Jeremiah.

5.   1. Sheshbazzar. 2. Ezra. 3. Nehemiah.

6.   a.   The events of the Book of Esther occurred in Persia during the reign of Ahasuerus, the fourth king of the Persian Empire (486-465 BC).
      b.   The events of Esther occur chronologically between Ezra chapters six and seven.

7.   The Book of Esther provides two important historical markers: Esther 1:3—Ahasuerus's 3rd year and Esther 3:7—Ahasuerus's 12th year.

8.   1.   The Book of Esther provides a description of the origin and administration of the feast of Purim, the sacred Jewish holiday.
      2.   The Book of Esther reminded the returning exiles of God's faithfulness.
      3.   The Book of Esther teaches that God's providential care overrules all things in all lands.

9.   King Ahasuerus held a royal banquet in the Persian capital of Susa for all princes, nobles, their attendants, and army officers. (Note: It is likely that these key political and military leaders did not come to Susa simultaneously, but came and left in order to provide political and military supervision in the event of a possible uprising. Secular history tells us that Ahasuerus was planning a military campaign against Greece to avenge his father's defeat at the battle of Marathon [490 BC]. Ahasuerus likely held the banquet to plan a military strategy with his officers and to demonstrate his sufficient financial resources for undertaking a massive military maneuver.)

10. 1.   King Ahasuerus held a banquet for the people of Susa in the court of the garden of the palace (Es. 1:5). The banquet lasted seven days.

      2.   Queen Vashti held a banquet for the women of the palace. (Note: Although the text does not give a specific reason for the banquets, it is possible that the banquets were held for the people who helped the king and queen host the various guests during the previous 180 days.)

11. a.   Ahasuerus wanted to display her beauty to the people and the princes.

      b.   The king became very angry, and his wrath burned against her (i.e., he allowed his anger to continue [v. 12]). He asked the wise men of Persia what should be done about her refusal to honor his request (vv. 13-15).

12. a. 1.   He is defenseless. An ancient city without walls was an easy target for an enemy. In the same way, an individual who cannot control his spirit is an easy target for Satan.

          2.   He is insecure and fearful. Citizens of an unwalled city must feel a degree of apprehension and fear knowing that they are easy prey for enemy attack. Their fear influences their actions and their ability to live confidently. A person who has not learned to control his spirit is often insecure and fearful because he knows his vulnerablility to Satan's attack. His insecurity and fear often cause him to avoid certain situations in life that could cause him to "lose his cool." Instead of allowing God to give him control over his temptation, he avoids situations that may upset him.

          3.   He lives in defeat. Like an unwalled city that must be willing to surrender at any time, the man who has no control over his spirit lives in defeat rather than experiencing the victory that Christ wants to give him (Ro. 8:31-39).

      b.   Answers will vary.

13. a. 1.   He should not have allowed his anger to continue to burn within him (v. 2). His continuing state of wrath indicates that he was focusing on Vashti's error rather than his insensitivity toward his wife.

          2.   He should not have attempted to solve the problem until he gained control over his emotions (vv. 13 ff.).

          3.   He should have attempted to resolve the problem personally without soliciting the counsel of others (vv. 13 ff.).

          4.   He should not have prejudiced the wise men by asking what should be done with *Queen Vashti*. The manner in which he approached the problem—and their counsel—dictated their response to him.

      b.   She could have appealed to her husband in private. This would have provided the opportunity to withdraw his request graciously without embarrassment. (Note: There is nothing in the passage or the Hebrew grammar to indicate that Ahasuerus wanted Vashti to appear naked or dance lewdly before the king and his guests. Some scholars believe the queen was pregnant with Artaxerxes

(Ahasuerus's son who became the next king) and did not want to appear before the drunken king and his guests.

14. a. A Christian should not accept counsel if it does not agree with the Word of God.
    b. The counsel that a believer receives must agree with the Word of God.

15. The king was to appoint overseers in all the provinces of the kingdom who would gather beautiful young women from throughout the empire and bring them to the Persian capital where they would be placed in the custody of Hegai, the eunuch in charge of the king's harem. The women would be given oil of myrrh for six months and spices and cosmetics for another six months. At the end of twelve months, the women would spend the night with the king. The woman who most pleased to the king would become the new queen.

16. 1. The king's attendants recommended a plan that appointed overseers to gather every beautiful young woman to Susa to become part of the king's harem (v. 3).
    2. Esther was taken to the king's palace, into the custody of Hegai (v. 8). Both verses indicate that this was not a voluntary surrender or "beauty contest."

17. Although Mordecai and Esther possessed a faith in God and trusted Him to protect His people (cf. Es. 4:14), it appears that their immersion into the secular environment in which they lived had caused them to become weak in faith. Under the leadership of Sheshbazzar, Ezra, and Nehemiah, many of the Jews had returned to Palestine as the prophets had commanded. Those who remained behind in Persia seemed to be more concerned about their personal interests than obeying the direct command of the Lord.

18. Answers will vary.

Study # 2a/b   *"If I Perish, I Perish"*

1. Esther continued to honor and obey Mordecai after she became queen. This indicates that she had not lost sight of her family roots amidst the opulence of palace living.

2. 1. God ordained Mordecai to be the one told about the plot to kill the king.
    2. God caused the king and his palace officials to forget about Mordecai's good deed. If Mordecai had been rewarded for his loyalty to the king at the time, he would not have been honored later, at Haman's humiliation.

3. a. 1. God sometimes moves His people into specific locations so that He can use them at a future date.

        2. God does not always reveal to His servants the reason why He directs them into the specific position or responsibility. Other answers could apply.

    b. Christians should be willing to trust God to direct their lives. They should resist the temptation to become anxious or worry about what God is doing. They should also realize that He might not reveal to them the specific purpose or ministry He wants them to fulfill.

4. a. The Amalekites attacked the Israelite stragglers at the rear who were faint and weary and did not fear the Lord. (Note: A spiritual application can be easily drawn from this unfortunate historical situation: Satan attacks spiritual stragglers in the church who do not fear God.)

    b. God told the Israelites to destroy the Amalekites as soon as they had become established in the Promised Land. Although God instructed them not to forget to do this, they did not obey Him.

5. a. Saul was injured in battle and tried to kill himself by leaning on his own spear (v. 6). (Note: This was probably an attempt to avoid being tortured by his enemies.) Apparently he did not have enough strength and asked an Amalekite to take his life; the Amalekite agreed to Saul's request and killed him. Ultimately, Saul was killed by the same people God commanded him to destroy.

    b. Answers will vary.

6. Death. Although every person will face physical death, sinful conduct in a specific area of the believer's life (e.g., his personal relations, life goals, finances, thoughts, etc.) will cause death to occur in that area (i.e., the forfeiture of God's peace, grace and blessing in the particular area of violation). When Christ said that we might have abundant life (cf. Jn. 10:10), He was referring to a quality of life resulting from submitting to God's Word rather than simply an eternal home in heaven.

7. Answers will vary but could include: 1. "It is the law." 2. "Everyone is bowing down." 3. "If I don't bow down, I might lose my position and won't be able to continue to help Esther." 4. "If I don't bow down, I will not be a good example of humility and submission to authority."

8. a. 1. Both Ahasuerus and Haman became very angry (Es. 1:12, 3:5).

        2. Both men allowed their anger to continue (Es. 1:12, 3:6).

        3. Both men did not attempt to resolve their problem by going directly to the person who offended them (Es. 1:13, 3:8).

        4. Both men decided to resolve the problem by getting rid of the other person (Es. 1:21, 3:8).

        5. Both men turned a relatively small problem into a national scandal (Es. 1:12-22, 3:5-11).

      6.   Both men eventually regretted their decisions but for different reasons (cf. Es. 2:1; 7:10).

  b. 1.   Leaders will often attract followers that have the same attributes (strengths and weaknesses) as themselves.

      2.   Leaders usually are unable to see character weaknesses in their followers because they have not recognized weaknesses in their own lives.

      3.   Followers tend to resolve problems in the same manner as their superiors.

      4.   Having a position of authority does not automatically mean that a person has virtuous character.

      5.   Having a position of authority does not mean that a person naturally knows how to resolve interpersonal conflicts. Other answers could apply.

9. a. 1.   Ahasuerus did not even inquire about whom Haman wanted to destroy. It is obvious that he did not really care about his subjects.

      2.   He told Haman to do whatever he wanted without questioning him about other specific details of his plan (Es. 3:11).

      3.   Subsequent to the proclamation of Ahasuerus's edict to kill the Jews, the king and Haman sat down to drink while the city of Susa was in confusion (Es. 3:15).

  b. Answers will vary. There continues to be an increase of individuals who possess poor moral character in positions of significant social influence (e. g., politics, athletics, academia, etc.). The willingness of the public to give silent endorsement of people of little character continues to erode the moral fiber of the nation. The continuing de-emphasis on personal character as a requirement for political office has enabled many unqualified individuals to become elected officials. It is almost inevitable that a man's morality will dictate the decisions he makes in public office (i.e., his votes, his choice of staff, etc.). To say that an individual can be a good politician, even though he is a man of poor moral quality, fails to take into account the Biblical truth that righteousness exalts a nation (Pro. 14:34).

10. Esther summoned one of her servants to determine the exact nature of Mordecai's problem.

11. a. 1.   Mordecai told the servant to tell Esther all that happened to him (v. 7).

      2.   Mordecai told the servant to tell Esther the exact amount of money Haman promised to give the king's treasuries for the destruction of the Jews (v. 7).

      3.   Mordecai gave the servant a copy of the king's edict detailing Haman's plan (v. 8). Mordecai told Hathach to show Esther and explain the problem to her.

  b. Mordecai ordered Esther to go to the king, implore his favor, and plead for her people.

12.   Esther told Mordecai (through Hathach) that she could not approach the king because she might die if he was unwilling to give her an audience.

13. a.   1.   Mordecai told Esther she would not escape death even though she lived in the king's palace (v. 13).

              2.   Mordecai told Esther that if she remained silent, deliverance would arise from another place (v. 14).

              3.   Mordecai told Esther that if she remained silent and deliverance came from another place, she and her immediate family would perish. God's sovereign plan is not thwarted by man's individual failure. An individual's failure to obey God can be the cause of His personal judgment upon the person even in the midst of God's victory (e.g., Samson [Ju. 16:28-31]).

              4.   Mordecai told Esther that she possibly attained royalty for the very purpose of saving her people (v. 14).

    b.   Esther wanted Mordecai to assemble all the Jews in Susa and have them fast for three days. Esther would fast for the same period and then present herself before the king to ask for his help. (Note: Although prayer is not mentioned, it is probably assumed in her request.)

14.   **"If I perish, I perish."**

Study #3a/b   *How the Mighty Are Fallen*

1.   **"What is your petition, Queen Esther? It shall be granted you. And what is your request, – up to half the kingdom?" It shall be done!"**

2.   This is likely an idiomatic expression meaning that Esther could request whatever she desired, and her request would be granted, within all possible reason.

3. a.   Christians are to fervently love one another from the heart. The Greek word for "fervent" (*ektenos*) means intensely and earnestly. The verbal form of the word means "to stretch out the hand;" thus it means to reach out earnestly to others with the love of Christ.

    b.   Answers will vary.

4.   1.   He should confess his avoidance of another believer to God as sin and accept His forgiveness.

       2.   If the individual is fairly certain that the person he has been avoiding is not aware of being avoided by the other person, he should begin to love the person according to the Biblical pattern.

       3.   If the other person is aware that the individual has been avoiding him, the individual should go to that person, confess his sin, and seek to love him according to the Biblical pattern.

5. Esther's preparation of the banquet meal indicates that she had stepped out in faith and was trusting God to move in the heart of the king to grant her request. It also indicates that three days of fasting (and prayer) had given her a confidence that she did not previously possess.

6. 1. She told the king that she had a specific issue in mind (**"my petition"**).
    2. She told him that she had a specific request to make (**"tomorrow I will do as the king has said"**).
    3. She told him that she would tell the king what was on her heart the following evening (**"tomorrow I will do as the king says"**).

7. 1. Haman boasted about all his riches (v. 11).
    2. Haman boasted about the number of sons he had (v. 11).
    3. Haman boasted about his honors from King Ahasuerus (v. 11).
    4. Haman boasted about His quick promotions, faster than the other princes and servants in the kingdom (v. 11).
    5. Haman boasted about his exclusive invitation to a royal banquet with the king and queen (v. 12).

8. a. 1. **"Yet all this avails me nothing."**
    b. A. Solomon said the only reward he had for all his selfish labor was temporary satisfaction (v. 10). When he continued to evaluate his efforts and the resulting pleasure that he derived from his exertion, he came to the conclusion that all his labor was vanity or futility and striving after the wind (v. 11). What he meant was that his efforts did not produce lasting satisfaction. Just as the wind is elusive and chasing after it is futile, it is vanity to try to gain lasting satisfaction from selfish pursuits. Solomon also said that it is impossible to have lasting joy apart from God (Ecc. 2:24-26).
    c. Answers will vary.

9. 1. Zeresh and his friends counseled Haman to eliminate the problem (Mordecai) rather than dealing with his own sinful attitude.
    2. They disregarded the continuing negative effects of a guilty conscience that Haman would have experienced from the murder of Mordecai. They told Haman to hang Mordecai and then go joyfully to the banquet with Esther and the king. This would have been a difficult task for even someone as morally corrupt as Haman.

10. a. 1. King Ahasuerus raised his golden scepter, indicating his acceptance of Esther's intrusion (Es. 5:2).
   2. The king accepted Esther's invitation to a banquet she prepared (Es. 5:5-6). Circumstances (administrative affairs, etc.) could have prevented him from accepting her invitation.
   3. The king did not become impatient when Esther did not reveal her problem during the first banquet (Es. 5:8).
   b. 1. The king could not sleep on this particular night (v. 1).
   2. The king chose to have the official government records (chronicles) read as compared to some other form of entertainment (v. 1).
   3. The particular servant providentially brought the specific chronicle in which the events of Mordecai's good deed were recorded (v. 1).
   4. The servant happened to read the particular portion of the chronicle record that spoke of Mordecai's heroics.
   5. The king remained awake during the time that the record was read, despite the late hour (vv. 1-3).
   6. Mordecai had not previously been rewarded for his efforts (v. 3).
   7. The king realized that Mordecai had not been rewarded for his efforts to save the king, and he chose to reward him. The king could have chosen not to reward Mordecai because of the amount of elapsed time since the event.

11. 1. Blindness to the noble efforts of others. Haman could not envision the king delighting in any other person.
   2. Humiliation. Haman was humiliated before Mordecai and the people of the city. Other answers could apply.

12. a. They believed that the strange events were a sign that Haman would not be able to defeat Mordecai if he was of Jewish origin. Furthermore, they believed that Haman would surely fall before him (presumably a reference to death).
   b. There is no objective basis or authority from which to evaluate the various signs. The final source of authority becomes the mind of man. The fatalistic approach to evaluating the various "abnormalities" of life (luck, chance, fate, etc.) is a result of a failure to acknowledge the person and sovereignty of God. The fatalist believes that life has a prescribed administrative order that does not make sense to man because it is unknowable. While it is true that God does not reveal all things to His people, it is also true that He acts according to His character that is revealed in His word. This allows believers to understand and predict many of the things in life. Those that cannot be understood from a human perspective can be accepted as being part of the sovereign plan of an omniscient God.

13. Esther said that her people had been sold (possibly a reference to Haman's original offer to the king [cf. Es. 3:9]) to be destroyed, to be killed, and to be annihilated (Es. 7:4). She said that she would not have bothered the king if she and her people had been sold into physical slavery.

14. a.   Haman became terrified before the king and queen (Es. 7:6). When Ahasuerus went outside to contemplate what to do, Haman fell on the couch where Esther had been reclining and begged the queen for his life (Es. 7:7). The Jewish commentator, Dr. S. Goldman said, "The arrogant bully became, as usual in the face of disaster, a whining coward."

    b.   God's judgment will be merciless to those who have shown no mercy. The manner in which a person deals with the failures of others here on earth will affect God's judgment of that person in heaven.

15.   The servant Harbonah seemed to quickly report to the king of a place ready to execute Haman—his own gallows. Harbonah also testified that Mordecai had spoken well on behalf of the king. These instances indicate that Mordecai's unwillingness to pay homage to Haman was isolated to him alone rather than rebellion against all Gentile authority.

16. a.   Jacob's sons killed an animal and used part of it (the blood) to deceive their father.

    b.   The firstborn son of Pharaoh and other Egyptians were killed.

    c.   Answers will vary.

Study #4a/b   The Providence of God

1.   Ahasuerus gave Haman's signet ring to Mordecai, which meant that Mordecai became the new prime minister of Persia. Mordecai's new position allowed him to conduct official business in the king's name (cf. Es. 3:10).

2.   In this second instance, the king's scepter was extended after Esther's emotional plea (v. 4). In the first instance, the king's scepter had been extended to Esther at the time of her entrance into the king's court but before she spoke to the king. Likely, the king extended his scepter to encourage her to rise from her prostrate position before she continued to speak.

3.   According to Persian (and Median) law, a law could not be revoked (Dan. 6:8, 12). King Ahasuerus gave Mordecai the power to initiate new laws and encouraged him to negate the power of the first edict by enacting a law, which would allow the Jews to defend themselves.

4.   1.   The people of Susa, both Jews and Gentiles, shouted and rejoiced (v. 15). Obviously, this does not include those who led the military attack several months later (cf. Es. 9:6-15).   2.   The Jews living in Susa experienced joy and some degree of relief ("light" [v. 16]). The Jews felt honored that Mordecai had been chosen prime minister.   3.   Throughout the rest of the kingdom, the Jewish people were joyful because of the recent change of events. They feasted and held a holiday to celebrate their good fortune.

5. 1. The ancient cities of Canaan that were located where Jacob and his family lived (Gen. 35:1-6). Bethel is the only city specifically named (v. 6).
   2. Jericho and all the inhabitants of the land (i.e., of Canaan, which was the land immediately west of the Jordan River [Jos. 2:1-11]).
   3. The entire land of Canaan stretching west to the Mediterranean Sea, including the coastal plains and the hill country (land of the Canaanites and the Amorites [Jos. 5:1]).

6. a. 1. Some of the Israelites hid in caves, thickets, cliffs, cellars and pits (v. 6).
      2. Other Israelites followed Saul, trembling (v. 7).
      3. Others continued to desert because military assistance did not arrive (v. 8).
      4. King Saul took matters into his own hands and offered a sacrifice to God that he was not allowed to offer (vv. 8).
   b. 1. The people who were with Saul rallied (v. 20).
      2. The Israelites who had previously defected to the Philistines turned back to fight along with Israel (v. 21).
      3. The Israelites who had hidden themselves in caves and other places came out of hiding to join the battle (v. 22).

7. a. 1. The unsaved were convicted of their sinfulness before God (Acts 2:37).
      2. The people greatly wondered (Acts 3:11).
      3. The unsaved were grieved because of the apostles' teaching (Acts 4:1-3).
      4. The people marveled (Acts 4:13).
      5. The people did not want anything to do with the church even though they held the new believers in high esteem (Acts 5:13).
   b. Answers will vary.

8. a. If a man does not understand that his wife needs his undivided attention when she shares a story, his frustration will often make him into a poor listener. His assumption that there is no specific point to the conversation could easily offend his wife. The wife might then be tempted to withdraw emotionally from her husband over a period of time, which will eventually lead to greater problems in the marriage. On the other hand, if the wife does not understand how a man normally communicates, she might misinterpret his abruptness as an unwillingness to share his life with her. Both men and women should learn to communicate in a manner consistent with the pattern revealed in the Bible.
   b. Both men and women need to understand and apply the Biblical pattern of effective communication. This means that men need to voluntarily provide details when communicating with a woman. On the other hand, women need to learn to state the main point at the beginning of the conversation before providing additional details as necessary. (Note: Perhaps women would be more apt to state the main point at the beginning of a conversation if men were better listeners.)

9. The original casting of the lot by Haman gave the Jews twelve months from the original edict until the final encounter with their enemies. This was probably the maximum amount of time that the casting of the lot would allow.

10. It is important to remember that the second edict gave the Jews only the right to defend themselves. It is likely that Haman's ten sons wanted to avenge the death of their father. The fact that the fighting in Susa took two days, as compared to only one in the rest of the provinces, indicates that the hatred for the Jews was more intense in Susa than anywhere else.

11. 1. The writer likely wanted to emphasize that financial gain did not motivate the conflict.
    2. It is also possible that the writer wanted to demonstrate a sharp contrast between the actions of Saul, who took the best of the animals but spared Agag (cf. 1 Sam. 15:15-23), and the Persian Jews.

12. a. Mordecai wanted to be sure that the Jewish people would not fail to celebrate the victory over their enemies (Es. 9:27). He wanted the two days of battle and the victory to be remembered annually so that their deliverance would not fade from their descendants' memory (Es. 9:28).
    b. The feast is named after the Hebrew word for the casting of the lot (Heb. *pur*). Haman cast the lot to determine the specific day on which he and his followers would attempt to annihilate every Jew in the Persian Empire. This specific day became the day on which the Jews were providentially delivered from their enemies.

13. Christians must communicate the real meaning of a tradition to the next generation. The communication should be done patiently and diligently so that the following generation understands the true significance of the celebration. The next generation should also be instructed about their responsibility to communicate the underlying reason for the celebration and the importance of the tradition.

14. a. 1. Mordecai became greater and greater (Es. 9:4).
       2. He continued to seek the welfare of the whole nation (Es. 10:3).
    b. Answers will vary.

15. Answers will vary.

The Final Exam

Every person will eventually stand before God in judgment – The Final Exam.

The Bible says, ***"And as it is appointed for men to die once, but after this the judgment" (Hebrews 9:27).***

May I ask you a question? *"If you died today, do you know for certain that you would go to heaven?"* I do not ask you if you are religious or if you are a church member; nor do I ask if you have had some encounter with God—a meaningful, spiritual experience. I do not even ask you if you believe in God or angels, or if you are trying to live a good life. The question I am asking you is this: *"If you died today, do you know for certain that you would go to heaven?"*

When you die, you will stand alone before God in judgment. You will either be saved for all eternity or you will be separated from God for all eternity in what the Bible calls the lake of fire (Romans 14:12; Revelations 20:11-15). Tragically, many religious people who believe in God are not going to be accepted by Him when they die.

> ***"Many will say to Me in that day, `Lord, Lord, have we not prophesied in Your name, cast out demons in Your name, and done many wonders in Your name?' And then I will declare to them, `I never knew you. Depart from Me, you who practice lawlessness!'" (Matthew 7:22-23)***

God loves you and wants you to go to heaven (John 3:16; 2 Peter 3:9). If you are not sure where you will spend eternity, you are not prepared to meet God. God wants you to know for certain that you will go to heaven.

> ***"Behold, now is the accepted time; behold, now is the day of salvation. (2 Corinthians 6:2).***

The words **"behold"** and **"now"** are repeated because God wants you to know that you can be saved today. You do not need to hear those terrible words, ***"Depart from Me..."!***

Jesus Himself said, ***"You must be born again"*** (John 3:7). These are not the words of a pastor, a church or a particular denomination; they are the words of Jesus Christ Himself. You <u>must</u> be born again (saved from eternal damnation) before you die; otherwise, it will be too late when you die! You can know for certain today that God will accept you into heaven when you die.

> ***"These things I have written to you who believe in the name of the Son of God, that you may <u>know</u> that you have eternal life ..." (1 John 5:13)***

The phrase, *" you may know"* means that you can know for certain before you die that you will go to heaven. To be born again, you must understand and believe (this means to place your faith in) four essential spiritual truths. These truths are trustworthy, right from the Bible, not some man-made religious traditions.

Now let's consider these four essential spiritual truths:

1St Essential Spiritual Truth. <u>The Bible teaches that you are a sinner and separated from God.</u>

No one is righteous in God's eyes, including you. To be righteous means to be totally without sin, even a single act.

> *"There is none righteous, no, not one; There is none who understands; There is none who seeks after God. They have all turned aside; They have together become unprofitable; There is none who does good, no, not even one." (Romans 3:10-12).*

> *"For all have sinned and fall short of the glory of God" (Romans 3:23).*

Look at the words God uses to show that all men are sinners – **none, not one, all turned aside, not even one**. God is making a point – all men are sinners, including you. No man is good (perfectly without sin) in His sight. The reason is sin.

Have you ever lied, lusted, hated someone, stolen anything or taken God's name in vain, even once? These are sins. One sin makes you a sinner and unrighteous in God's eyes.

Are you willing to admit to God that you are a sinner? If you are, then tell Him right now you have sinned. You can say the words in your heart or out loud; it doesn't matter. But be honest with God. Check the box if you admit you are a sinner.

> ❑ *God, I admit I am a sinner in your eyes.*

2nd Essential Spiritual Truth. <u>The Bible teaches that you cannot save yourself.</u>

Man's sin is a very serious problem in the eyes of God. Your sin separates you from God, both now and for all eternity unless you are born again.

> *"For the wages of sin is death ..." (Romans 6:23).*

> *"And you He made alive, who were dead in trespasses and sins" (Ephesians 2:1).*

Wages are payments a person earns for what he or she has done. Your sin has earned you the wages of death, which means separation from God. If you die without ever having been born again, you will be separated from God after death.

You cannot save yourself or purchase your entrance into heaven. The Bible says that man is, *"... not redeemed with corruptible things, like gold or silver ..."* (1 Peter 1:18). If you owned all the money in the world, you could not buy your entrance into heaven nor can you buy your way into heaven with good works.

> *"For by grace you are saved through faith, and that <u>not of yourselves</u>, it is the gift of God, <u>not of works lest any man should boast</u>"* (Ephesians 2:8-9).

The Bible says salvation is, *"not of yourselves"* *"not of works, lest any man should boast."* Salvation from eternal judgment cannot be earned by doing good works. It is a gift of God. There is nothing you can do to purchase your way into heaven because you are already unrighteous in God's eyes.

If you understand you cannot save yourself, tell God right now that you are a sinner, are separated from Him, and are incapable of saving yourself. Check the box below if you admit that.

> ❑ *God, I admit that I am separated from You because of my sin. I realize that I cannot save myself.*

3rd Essential Spiritual Truth. <u>**The Bible teaches that Jesus Christ died on the cross to pay the complete penalty for your sin and to purchase a place in heaven for you.**</u>

Jesus Christ, the sinless Son of God, lived a perfect life, died on the cross, and rose from the dead to pay the penalty for your sin and to purchase a place in heaven for you. He died on the cross on your behalf, in your place, as your substitute, so you do not have to go to hell. Jesus Christ is the only acceptable substitute for your sin.

> *"For He [God, the Father] made Him [Jesus] who knew [committed] no sin to be sin for us, that we might become the righteousness of God in Him"* *(2 Corinthians 5:21).*

> *"I [Jesus] am the way, the truth, and the life No one comes to the Father except through Me"* *(John 14:6).*

> *"Nor is there salvation in any other, for there is no other name under heaven given among men by which we must be saved"* *(Acts 4:12).*

Jesus Christ is your only hope and means of salvation. Because you are a sinner, you cannot pay for your sins; but Jesus paid the penalty for your sins by dying on the cross in your place. Friend, there is salvation in no one else – not angels, not some religious leader, not even your religious good works. No religious act such as baptism, confirmation or joining a church can save you. There is no other way, no other name who can save you. Only Jesus Christ can save you. You must be saved by accepting Jesus Christ's substitutionary sacrifice for your sins, or you will be lost forever.

Do you see clearly that Jesus Christ is the only way to God in heaven? If you understand this truth, tell God that you understand and check the box below.

> ❑ *God, I understand that Jesus Christ died to pay the penalty for my sin. I understand that His death on the cross is the only acceptable sacrifice for my sins.*

4th Essential Spiritual Truth. <u>The Bible teaches that you must trust in Jesus Christ alone for eternal life and call upon Him to be your Savior and Lord</u>

Many religious people admit they have sinned. They believe Jesus Christ died for the sins of the world but they are not saved. Why? Thousands of moral, religious people have never completely placed their faith in Jesus Christ alone for eternal life. They think they must believe in Jesus Christ as a real person and do good works to earn their way to heaven. They are not trusting Jesus Christ alone. To be saved, you must trust in Jesus Christ alone for eternal life. Look at what the Bible teaches about trusting Jesus Christ alone for salvation.

> *"that if you confess with your mouth the Lord Jesus and believe in your heart that God has raised Him from the dead, <u>you will be saved</u>. For with the heart one believes unto righteousness, and with the mouth confession is made unto salvation . . . For there is no distinction between Jew or Greek, for the same Lord over all <u>is rich to all </u>who call upon Him. For <u>whoever calls on the name of the Lord shall be saved</u>" (Romans 10:9, 10, 12, 13).*

Do you understand what God is saying? To be saved or born again, you need to trust Jesus Christ <u>alone </u>for eternal life. Jesus Christ paid for your complete salvation. Jesus said, *"It is finished"* (John. 19:30). Jesus paid for your salvation completely when He shed His blood on the cross for your sin.

If you believe that God resurrected Jesus Christ, which proves God's acceptance of Jesus as a worthy sacrifice for man's sin, and you are willing to confess the Lord Jesus Christ as your Savior and Lord, master of your life, you will be saved.

Friend, right now God is offering you the greatest gift in the world. God wants to give you the <u>gift</u> of eternal life, the <u>gift </u>of His complete forgiveness for all your sins, and the <u>gift</u> of His unconditional acceptance into heaven when you die. Will you accept His free gift now, right where you are?

If you are unsure how to receive the gift of eternal life, review the essential spiritual truths:
1. You admitted you are a sinner.
2. You admitted your sin separates you from God you can't save yourself.
3. You realized that Christ is the only way to heaven – no other name can save you.
4. Now, you must call upon the Lord Jesus Christ to save your lost soul.

Ask Him right now to save you. Just take God at His word – He will not lie to you! This is the kind of simple faith you need to be saved. If you are still uncertain what to do, pray this prayer to God. Remember, the words must come from your heart.

God, I am a sinner and deserve to go to hell. Thank you, Jesus, for dying on the cross for me and for purchasing a place in heaven for me. Please forgive me for all my sins and take me to heaven when I die. I call on you, Jesus, right now to save me forever. Thank you for saving me now. Amen.

If you just asked Jesus Christ to save you in the best way you know how, God just saved you. He said in His Holy Word, *"Whoever calls upon the name of the Lord shall be saved" (Romans 10:13)* and the **whoever** includes you – it's that simple. God just gave you the gift of eternal life by faith. You have just been born again according to the Bible.

You will not come into eternal judgment, and you will not perish in the lake of fire – you are saved forever! Read this verse over carefully and let it sink into your heart.

> **"Most assuredly, I say to you, he who hears My word and believes in Him who sent Me has everlasting, and shall not come into judgment, but has passed from death into life."** (John. 5:24)

Final Questions:
- According to God's Holy Word (John. 5:24), not your feelings, what kind of life did God just give you? _____.
- What two words did God say at the beginning of the verse to assure you that He is not lying to you? _____ _____ .
- Are you going to come into judgment - YES or NO?
- Have you passed from spiritual death into life - YES or NO?

Friend, you have just been born again. You just became a child of God. We would like to help you grow in your new Christian life. We will send you a Spiritual Birth Certificate to remind you of your spiritual birthday and some Bible study materials to help you understand more about the Christian life.   To receive these helpful materials free of charge, photocopy the form below, fill it out and send it to us by mail or e-mail us at resources @LamplightersUSA.org.

Lamplighters Response Card
Lamplighters International, 6301 Wayzata Blvd, St. Louis Park, MN, USA 55416

❏ I just accepted Jesus Christ as my Savior and Lord on (date) _____, 200____
at _____.

❏ Please send me the Spiritual Birth Certificate and the Bible Study materials to help me grow as a Christian.

❏ I would like to begin attending a Bible-believing church in the area where I live. Please recommend some Bible-believing churches in the area where I live.

❏ I already know of a good Bible-believing church that I will be attending to help me grow as a new Christian.

Name _____

Address _____

City _____ State _____ Zip _____

Email address _____